If the Dawn is Late in Coming

Surviving Vilna and Vaivara

Ida Weisbaum Feinberg

And Maryann McLoughlin, Ph.D.

A project of the Holocaust Resource Center
of The Richard Stockton College of New Jersey

Published by:
ComteQ Publishing
A division of ComteQ Communications, LLC
P.O. Box 3046
Margate, New Jersey 08402
609-487-9000 • Fax 609-487-9099
Email: publisher@ComteQcom.com
Website: www.ComteQpublishing.com

ISBN10 0-9793771-5-3
ISBN13 978-0-9793771-5-0
Library of Congress Control Number: 2008922447

Book design by Ryan Schocklin, Stockton Graphics Department
Cover design by Sarah A. Messina

Printed in the United States of America
10 9 8 7 6 5 4 3 2 1

In memory of my
Beloved husband, Sender

Partisan Song

Zog nit keyn mol az du geyst dem letsten veg,
Khotsh himlen blayene farsthtelen bloye teg.
Never say you are walking your final road,
Though leaden skies conceal the days of blue.

Kumen vet nokh undzer oysgebenkte sha'ah,
S'vet a poyk ton undzer trot mir zaynen do!
The hour that we have longed for will appear,
Our steps will beat out like drums: We are here!

Fun grinem palmenland biz vaysen land fun shney,
Mir kumen on mit undzer payn, mit undzer vey.
From the green lands of palm trees to lands white with snow,
We are coming with our all pain and all our woe.

Un vu gefalen s'iz a shpritz fun undzer blut,
Shprotzen vet dort undzer gevurah, undzer mut.
Wherever a spurt of our blood has fallen to the ground,
There our might and our courage will sprout again.

S'vet di morgenzum bagilden undz dem haynt,
Un der nekhten vet farshvinden miten faynd.
The morning sun will shine on us one day,
Our enemy will vanish and fade away.

Nor oyb farzamen vet di zun in dem kayor,
Vi a parol zol geyn dos lid fun dor tsu dor.
But if the sun and dawn come too late for us, [1]
From generation to generation let them be singing this song.

Dos lid geshriben iz mit blut un nit mit blay,
S'iz nit keyn lidel fun a foygel oyf der fray,
This song is written in blood not in pencil-lead.
It is not sung by the free-flying birds overhead,

Dos hot a folk tsvishen falendike vent,
Dos lid gezungen mit naganes in di hent!
But a people stood among collapsing walls,
And sang this song with pistols in their hands! [2]

Acknowledgements

I thank Ida Weisbaum Feinberg for agreeing to tell her story. She had rarely told her story before, not even to the Shoah Foundation. Ida finds it very difficult to talk about this tragic and horrible period in her life from 1941 when the Germans occupied Vilna until she was liberated in 1945. She is telling her story now as a legacy for her son, grandsons, and future generations as well as for students.

I thank her family, especially Lee and Bonnie, for helping with some details to complete the memoir.

I want to thank The Richard Stockton College of New Jersey's General Studies Department, in particular, Dr. G. Jan Colijn, for his support of the Holocaust Resource Center's projects. I also appreciate what Stockton's Graphics Department—under the guidance of Julie Bowen, the director; Sarah Messina, the cover designer; and Ryan Schocklin, the book designer—has done to bring this memoir to publication.

None of these memoirs would be possible without the help of Gail Rosenthal, Supervisor of Stockton's Holocaust Resource Center. The "Writing as Witness" Program was her inspiration.

Maryann McLoughlin, Ph.D.
January 2008

Table of Contents

Lee's Preface

The Holocaust was a horrific and defining time for the world—not only during the war, but also for generations to come. Those who lived and survived the Holocaust passed down experiences that affect us all—in particular their offspring and extended families. Some survivors were fortunate to be able to move forward and enjoy a happy and productive life. Others just survived. Some were effusive in sharing what they lived through. The silence of others has an equally compelling effect. Out of courage or fear, strength of will or sheer happenstance, those that survived play an important role in history—the ability and responsibility to impart the fierce determination to "never forget." That is why my mother, my sons, and I are proud to share my parents' stories.

To be a child—an only child—of surviving Holocaust parents is to be a child of privilege, resentment, many questions, and most critically, of a constant determination to succeed, regardless of the task or aspiration.

My parents' lives essentially took a hiatus when "the war" broke out, and they never again regained the footing and passion they enjoyed as children and young adults. After all, they made it through one of the most horrific experiences a human being can possibly imagine. And as fortunate as they were to survive, that's how frozen in their youth they became.

Don't misunderstand. These thoughts are not bitter ones, and they're not self-pity. They are actually reflective of the strength, determination, and character that have driven me to my personal and professional achievements in life. I consider myself a better person because of the lessons learned from their survival, their fears, and their history.

I can honestly say that I am who I am, and, by extension, my sons are who they are, because of what Sender and Ida were subjected to. All in all, a happy and positive consequence born out of a nightmare.

Lee Feinberg
December 2007

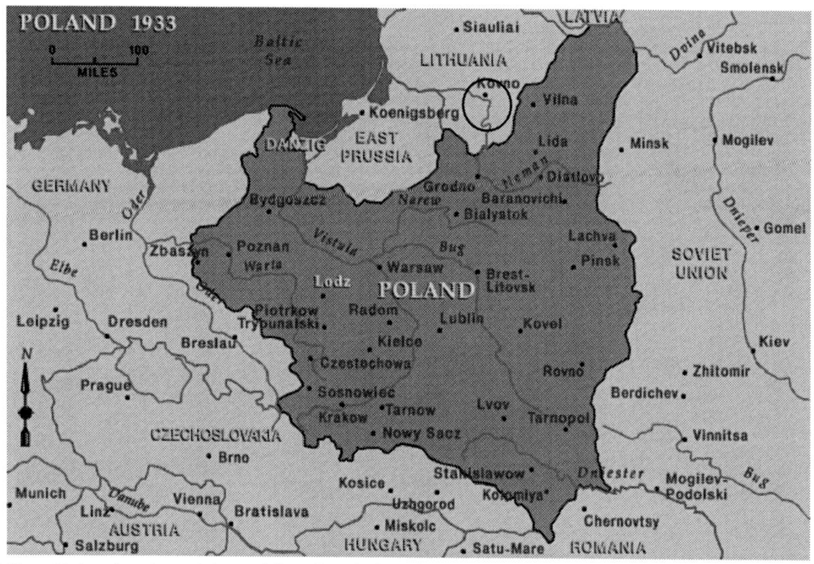

Vilna, Poland, where Ida and her family lived. ushmm.org

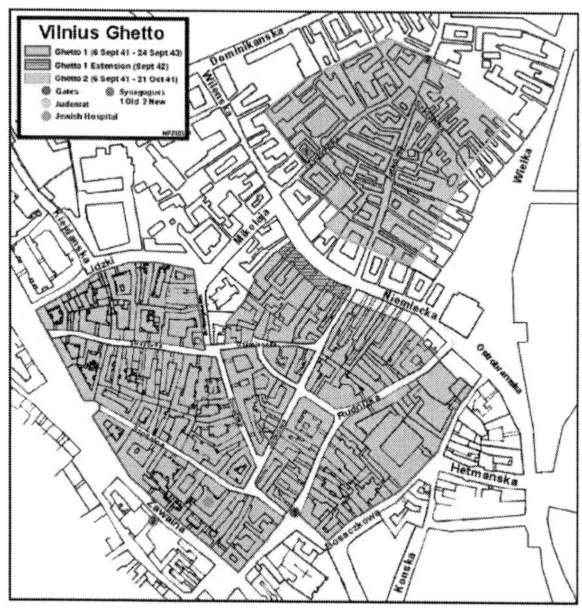

Ida was in both Vilna Ghettos, #1 and #2.
deathcamps.org

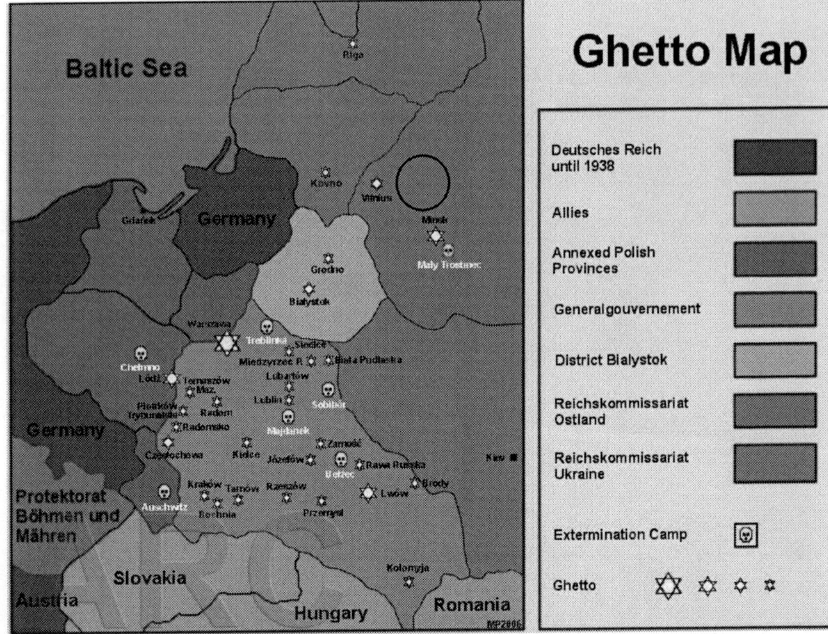

Polish Ghettos and Death Camps *deathcamps.org*

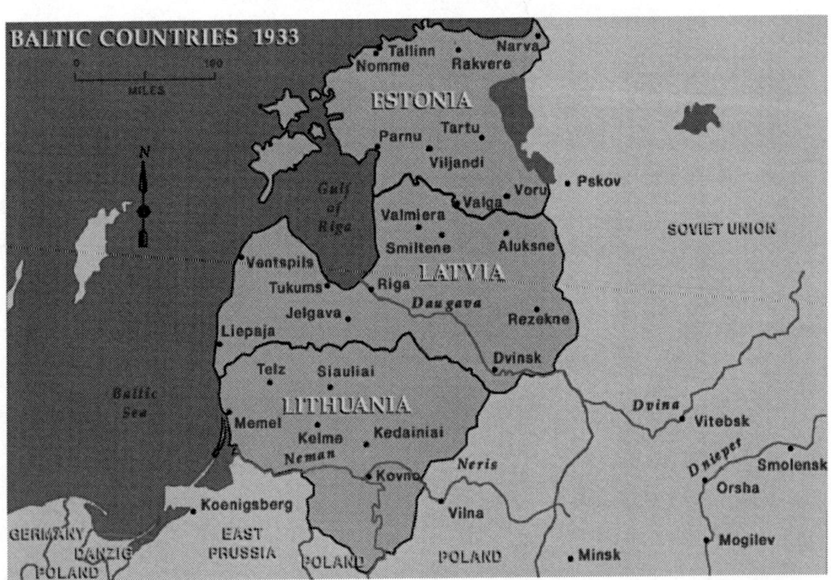

Ida was sent to a slave labor camp in northeast Estonia—to Vaivara, near the Estonian-Soviet border. During the death march from Vaivara, Ida walked along the Baltic Coast toward Germany. *ushmm.org*

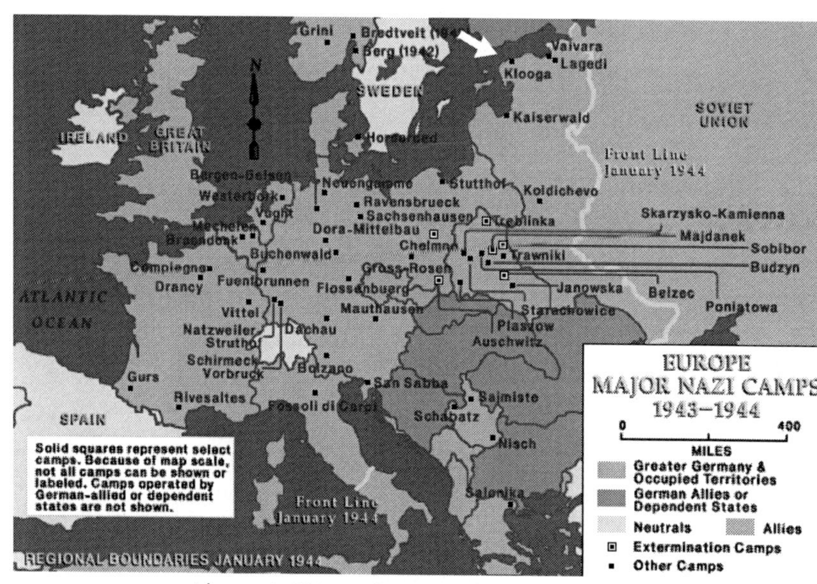

Ida was in Vaivara Concentration Camp. See arrow.

Vilna (Vilnius) is now the capital of Lithuania. cia.gov

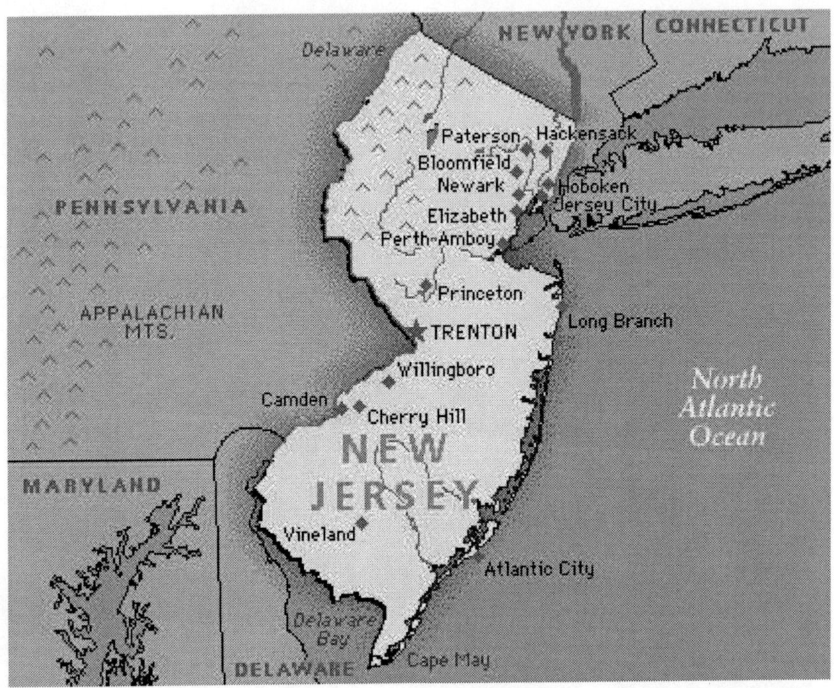

In 1949, Ida and Sam moved to Vineland, New Jersey, and bought a chicken farm.
greenwichmeantime.com

Chapter One
The Jerusalem of Lithuania

Generations of my family had lived in The Jerusalem of Lithuania—the beautiful and cosmopolitan Vilna.

Vilna (also known as Vilnius), presently the capital of Lithuania and one of the country's oldest cities, was founded in the fourteenth-century.[3] Vilna, stretches along both banks of the Neris River. Vilna was known as "a charming city, a multilayered and multilingual place harmoniously blending Medieval, Baroque, and Classical architecture, surrounded by pine forests and moist hills" (Venclova 1).

As you would expect with this blending of ethnic groups and languages, Vilna was especially well known for its culture. In the sixteenth-century one of the oldest universities in Eastern Europe was established—the Vilnius University, founded by the Jesuits. The university soon developed into one of the most important scientific and cultural centers of the region and the most notable scientific centre of the Polish-Lithuanian Commonwealth. From the fourteenth to the nineteenth century, the city rapidly developed. This development was expedited, in 1860, by the building of a railway, the first in Lithuania, which connected Vilna with St. Petersburg, Russia, and Warsaw, Poland.

Over the years, Vilna changed hands a number of times—once Polish, another time Russian or Lithuanian, and once Vilna was even seized by Napoleon.

During World War I (1914-1918), before I was born, Vilna was occupied by the Germans, by Kaiser Wilhelm II's troops, between 1915 and 1918.

After World War I, Poland and Lithuania both claimed Vilna. On February 16, 1918, the Lithuanian Council in Vilnius proclaimed an independent Lithuanian Republic. In 1920, the year I was born, Polish forces occupied Vilna, and by the autumn of 1920, Vilna and the region to which it belonged became part of northeastern Poland (then known as Wilna).

Ethnic Lithuanians were forced to leave the city and the use, in public, of the Lithuanian language was banned. Gradually Poles, Jews and non-Jews, made up a majority of the population of the city, with a small Lithuanian minority.

Pre-World War II, in 1931, Vilna's Jewish population was nearly 60,000, of a total population of 196,000, about thirty percent of the city's total. Vilnius had 105 synagogues and prayer houses. There were six daily Jewish newspapers. Yiddish was the language of choice. This beautiful and cosmopolitan city was then called "The Jerusalem of Poland." (neris.mii.lt; ushmm.org; deathcamps.org; jewishvirtuallibrary.org)

Chapter Two
Early Years

My parents, Wolf and Hanna Weisbaum, as well as my grandparents and great-grandparents, on both sides, had lived in Vilna for generations. My mother was an only child. On my father's side, however, I had aunts and uncles living in another part of town.

My father was an engineer for a flour mill, and my mother stayed at home, as many women did then, raising the children, my brother, Peter, and me. I was born on September 15, 1920, and Peter, in 1917.

We lived in a four-story apartment building on the bottom floor. My Grandmother Bela lived with us. Grandmother Bela was my mother's mother. When my grandfather died at a young age, Grandmother Bela came to live with us. She helped to raise me; she was my *Bubbe* (Yiddish: dear, beloved little grandmother).

Our next door neighbors were Polish but non-Jews. I was often in their home. I went there for holidays and weddings. During our holidays, such as *Purim* and Passover, we shared our dishes with them.

The children in the neighborhood, boys and girls, Jews and

non-Jews, played together. I went to public school for seven years. I could not go on to higher education because Jews were not permitted to attend high school or university because of the *numerus clausus*, a quota system.[4] In Poland, the quota was 10% for Jews. However, although I didn't attend higher education, I knew many languages: Polish, Yiddish, Hebrew, Lithuanian, and eventually German, Russian, and English.

After I finished school in 1934, I worked as a sales lady in a stationary shop, where they sold notepaper, envelopes, and stationary.

This was my life in Vilna—home, friends, and work—until September 19, 1939, when the Soviets occupied Vilna.

Chapter Three
The Russian Occupation

Under the terms of the German-Soviet Pact, [5] Vilna, along with the rest of eastern Poland, was occupied by Soviet forces in late September 1939. In October 1939, the Soviet Union transferred the Vilna region to Lithuania. The population of the city was about 200,000 at this time, including over 55,000 Jews. In addition, thousands of Jewish refugees from German-occupied Poland had found refuge in the city. Due to this influx of refugees, the Jewish population had swollen to at least 80,000 by June 1941. (ushmm.org; deathcamps.org)

The Soviet occupation of Vilna did not affect my family very much. In fact, many in the Red Army regarded us as comrades because some had the mistaken idea that all Jews were Bolsheviks (left-wing and sympathetic to Marxism). Therefore, for the most part, we continued to live our lives normally.

Chapter Four
Love and Marriage

In 1940, when I was twenty years old, my life was enriched. A neighbor had a luncheon, and there I met a man named Sender (later Sam) Fajnberg, a tailor, twenty-five years old, born in 1915. The next day Sender came to visit me, and I introduced him to my parents. My mother invited him to lunch for *Purim*.[6] *Purim* is a feast, a time for sweetness and joy, so it is fitting that I met Sender then. *Purim* also commemorates a victory over oppression, and Sender and I did prevail over the evil of the Nazis.

My father used to say that I could have done better, but Sender was good to me. We were married for almost sixty years!

I married Sender on September 14, 1940. A beautiful day! The sun shone brightly. We were married at my cousin's home. The *chuppah*[7] was outside, and the wedding luncheon was inside.

Vilna was not yet occupied by the Germans. At the time we did not know how soon the sun would cease to shine on the Jews.

Chapter Five
The German Occupation

Less than a year after our wedding, on June 22, 1941, under *Operation Barbarossa*, Germany attacked Soviet forces in Eastern Europe breaking the German-Soviet Pact of 1939. The *Wehrmacht* (German army) occupied Vilna on June 25, 1941, the third day after the invasion. Thinking that the Germans would treat them better than the Soviets had, many Lithuanians greeted the *Wehrmacht* with flowers. Jews, however, did not greet the *Wehrmacht* with flowers. We had heard of the Nazis' cruel treatment of other Jews—in Germany and Poland, wherever they occupied.

Therefore , we were not surprised by the first announcement from the German commander: "The German soldiers are coming to free the population from Communist bondage and the Jews must wear arm bands with a star of David; they must not leave their quarters; they must carry out the required work and yield their radio sets" (Ran 426).

In July 1941, the German military administration began issuing a series of anti-Jewish and anti-Communist decrees. On July 8, 1941, a decree was issued by the military commander Zenfenig,

"Beginning July 8, all Jews must wear on their right arms a white band of ten centimeters with a yellow circle and the letter 'J' (*Jude*). For disobedience—the death penalty" (Ran 427). On August 2, District Commissar Hans Hingst issued a decree ordering Jews to wear the yellow star: "Beginning August 2, all Jews must wear on their chests and on their backs a yellow star of David. For disobedience—the most severe punishment" (Ran 427).

Also in July 1941: Jews were forbidden to walk along the main streets and forbidden to use radios, public transportation, and public spaces. Shops could sell Jews food in only limited quantities. Jewish people were fired from their jobs. (deathcamps.org) Some Jews were hired for other work but their employers were instructed by Franz Mürer: "All enterprises that employ Jews should utilize them exclusively for hard physical labor and get the maximum out of them. Each conflict with a Jew should be turned over to me [Mürer] for handling" (Ran 429). Some used their new employment to help the people in the ghettos; "Twenty-two former doctors, lawyers, and merchants graduated from the courses for chimney sweeps. Together with the eighteen chimney cleaners they served the whole city—smuggled and established contacts with non-Jews" (Ran 438).

During July 1941, worse things began to happen. Jewish men continued to be abducted, grabbed on the streets, at their jobs, and in their homes. First the Germans took them to Lukiszki Prison (where Peter was taken in June 1941) and then to Ponary, a wooded area, ten kilometers outside the old town of Vilna.[8] In Ponary, *Einsatzgruppen* (mobile killing squads—SS and SD)[9] aided by Lithuanian auxiliaries (police and civil defense units) killed 5,000 Jewish men.

The Lithuanians collaborated with the *Einsatzgruppen* for several reasons. For many Lithuanians antisemitism was traditional; moreover, the Jews had been perceived as Bolsheviks, allied with the Russians, whom the Lithuanians hated for taking away their independence, so they collaborated with the Germans.

The killings at Ponary continued into August and September of 1941. Between August 31 and September 3, 1941, the Germans and Lithuanians killed another 3,500 Jews at Ponary (Abba Kovner, the Vilna partisan commander, witnessed this *Aktion*—the assembling of Jews to be taken away to be murdered).

During the German occupation, tens of thousands of Jews from Vilna and the surrounding area, as well as Soviet prisoners of war and others, such as Polish priests and those suspected of opposing the Germans, were massacred at Ponary. Even women and children were included in these numbers. In fact, Lithuania was the first occupied country in which Germans murdered Jewish women and children "on a massive scale." (Matthüs 24-38).

Chapter Six
Peter

I remember well that in late June of 1941, on a Saturday night, I saw the Germans marching into Vilna. At this time, I had been married for over a year. Sender and I were living in the building where my parents, Grandmother Bela, and Peter lived.

We were affected immediately by the occupation. The second day after the Germans occupied Vilna, on June 26, 1941, Peter walked out to visit a friend. While he was walking, the Germans rounded him up. They told my mother to bring a food package for Peter to the Lukiszki Jail. Mother and I brought this package to the jail. But we don't believe Peter ever received it. We think he was dead by then. We never saw Peter again. We believe that he was taken to Ponary and killed.

Chapter Seven
The Ghettos

We first heard the rumors of the establishment of a ghetto in Vilna in July 1941. The Germans, led by Hans Hingst, the district commissar, and Franz Mürer, the expert on "the Jewish question," ordered a *Judenrat* (a Jewish Council) to be formed. This council was supposed to control the ghetto and act as liaison between the Jewish ghetto inhabitants and the Germans. In early September of 1941, the rumors became a reality.

The Germans established two ghettos—Ghetto # 1 and Ghetto # 2, each enclosed by a wooden fence. Each ghetto had only one gate for entering and one for exiting—at opposite ends of the ghettos.

On September 6, 1941, Jews were ordered to leave their homes and move to the two ghettos. Many of those unable to find space were taken to Ponary. The average living space in the Vilna Ghetto was 1.5 to 2.0 meters, so some people slept in the streets. In addition to this over-crowding were the ramshackle housing and the lack of sanitation. This was a chaotic scene—the many Jewish families moving into these two small areas. In a few days those two ghettos were sealed.

Ghetto #2 lasted for only six weeks; I was there only briefly. Jews considered incapable of work were concentrated in ghetto # 2, about 10,000 people—orphans, sick, and the elderly. This smaller of the two ghettos lasted until October 1941, but long enough for German *Einsatzgruppen* detachments and Lithuanian auxiliaries to massacre those 10,000 Jews at Ponary. Thus ghetto # 2 was destroyed.

Ghetto # 1 was for craftsmen and workers with permits (The Germans distributed 3,000 yellow colored *Schein* or "Personal *Ausweis* [identity card]," which enabled the bearers to register on each *Schein* the other parent and two children). Sender and my father both had these *Scheine*.

About 29,000 Jews were forced to work in factories or in construction projects outside the ghetto. Some Jews were sent to labor camps in the Vilna region.

The SS or the Lithuanian police units came into the ghetto every day and seized people: at first a hundred, then *Aktionen* of a thousand a day. In these periodic killing operations, most of the ghetto's inhabitants were massacred at Ponary. By the end of 1941 over 35,000 of the ghetto inhabitants had been killed. For those who remained in the ghetto, there was fear, terror, and panic. There was grief over those taken. And there was slow starvation.

The rations that Jews received had a caloric value of 170-200 calories per day. (Seventy to eighty per cent of the women in the Vilna Ghetto ceased menstruating.[10]) A person who is not working should eat 1750 to 2,300 calories. A working person, according to the extent of the work, should eat 3,000, 4,000, or 5,000 calories. "If we had existed only on these food rations, a ration which was one-fifteenth of the food ration of an ordinary individual, and one twentieth of the food ration of a worker, the people of the ghetto would have died of starvation in one or two months" (Dr.Dworzecki). The *Judenrat* of Vilna Ghetto had decided early on not to allow the ghetto inhabitants to die of starvation. They used the slogan "Let there not be a hungry person in the ghetto" (*Es zol nisht zein kein hungriker in ghetto*). They also hung this slogan at the gate of the ghetto and set up a committee for public aid. They did not want anyone to starve. Thus they organized the smuggling of food.

"But even with the smuggling it was difficult to remain alive, for prices rose and a person then received only 800 to 1000 calories per day. Therefore, a lack of nutrition commenced, something which in German was euphemistically called 'general bodily weakness.'" (nizkor.org/ftp.cgi/people/e/eichmann.adolf/transcripts—interview with Dr. Dworzecki).

In addition to problems with nourishment, the ghetto dwellers also had to deal with diseases. Because of the overcrowding, dirt, cold, and undernourishment, a number of diseases were present in the ghetto. Skin rashes such as scabies, furuncles (boils caused by staph infections), skin inflammation, and scrofula spread, and other even more terrible diseases such as night blindness from a Vitamin A deficiency, tuberculosis, dysentery, and hunger edema in the last stages of starvation were problematic. However, the large number of physicians and medical personnel as well as the Jewish Hospital being included within the boundaries of the ghetto "prevented outbreaks of epidemic diseases that otherwise might have resulted in catastrophic death rates." Death rates were far higher than before the war, but "within certain limits, the health services of the Vilna Ghetto came close to being adequate." (Beinfeld 66-98)

Moreover, following the *Aktionen* of 1941 and early 1942, for a whole year—from the spring of 1942 until the spring of 1943—there were no mass *Aktionen*. Most people were employed inside or outside the ghetto, and an effort was made by the *Judenrat* to normalize conditions in the ghetto. The *Judenrat*'s policy, of rescue through work, *"Arbeit vershport blut"* (work saves blood) was based on the assumption that if the ghetto were productive, it would be worthwhile economically for the Germans to keep it going.

The dominant figure in the ghetto leadership was Jacob Gens, a controversial figure, who in July 1942 became *Judenrat* chairman.[11] Under Gens's leadership, the ghetto had schools, a rich cultural life—including colloquia in the home of Gens and poetry by Abraham Sutzkever—social-welfare institutions, and a medical care system. (motlc.learningcenter.wiesenthal.org)

Then, in the spring and summer of 1943, our situation deteriorated; nearby small ghettos and labor camps were liquidated. During *Aktionen* in August and early September of 1943, over seven thousand people were sent to labor camps in Estonia. After these deportations only twelve thousand people were left in the Vilna ghetto.

The Germans renewed the killings during the final liquidation of Ghetto # 1 on September 23 and 24, 1943. Thirty-seven hundred Jews were sent to the concentration camps in Estonia and Latvia; over four thousand children, the sick, and elderly were sent to Sobibor death camp; and several hundred were murdered at Ponary. The remaining Jews worked in nearby labor camps, worked disposing the bodies in Ponary, or had hidden outside the ghetto or in the Rudninkai and Naroch forests that surrounded Vilna. (ushmm.org; jewishvirtuallibrary.org)

Chapter Eight
My Family and the Ghettos

In September of 1941, a number of weeks after Peter was murdered, the Germans forced my parents, Wolf and Hanna Weisbaum, my *Bubbe* Bela, Sender, and me into the ghetto. [12] They rounded us up on Saturday, a Sabbath morning, just as we were sitting down to breakfast. They told us that we could only take a few possessions with us; we packed up our breakfast, we took gold, and we dressed in as many clothes as we could, but, in fact, we dropped much of what we had taken along the way. Our belongings were too heavy to carry. Besides it was very hot. We saw on both sides of the street the possessions that people had abandoned on their way to the ghetto.

So we left our home and our neighborhood. Our neighbors did not care what the Germans were doing to us. They never said good-bye or asked if they could help. Nothing! Perhaps they too were afraid of the Germans; nonetheless, they did nothing to help us or to let us know that they cared what happened to us.

People went into either ghetto at random. At first I was in Ghetto #2, separated from the rest of my family. I was there for only a few days when there was a selection, choosing people for either Ghetto #1 or Ghetto #2. Because Sender had a work permit (*Schein*), as his wife I was moved to Ghetto #1. My mother, father, my Grandmother Bela, and Sender's father, Labe, were also in Ghetto #1 because my father and Sender's father also had *Scheine* (plural of *Schein*).

Maybe a year later [possibly during the "Elders *Aktion*" of July 17, 1942], during one of the ghetto *Aktions*, my grandmother—my *Bubbe*—was taken. She left without even her shoes. She was only sixty years old. We never saw her again. She was probably taken to Ponary—murdered by the *Einsatzgruppen*.

Sender's father, Labe, died in the ghetto of cancer. Normally this would be a very sad thing, and, of course, his death was sad, but at least he was not deported to a death camp nor was he shot in the woods at Ponary.

Chapter Nine
The Ghetto Hospital

Efforts to protect the born and unborn children originated in the struggle between those who wanted to murder and those who wanted to save. It was an uneven struggle that left many child victims and few child survivors. Sometimes . . . . parent-child relationships lingered on and on, despite the brutal efforts to extinguish them. Perhaps, in more ways than we grasp, these primary relationships did endure, often reaching beyond unknown graves (Tec 17).

While I was in Ghetto #1, I became pregnant. Because of the Nazis and the situation in the ghetto, this was a bittersweet experience: sweet because Sender and I wanted a child; bitter because of the way Nazis treated Jewish mothers.

Nechama Tec, Holocaust survivor, scholar, and Professor of Sociology, writes,

> For Aryan German women, childbearing and child care were highly valued and encouraged by concrete rewards. In sharp contrast, Jewish procreation and motherhood were officially defined as political threats that would interfere with the basic goal of creating a pure Aryan world.
>
> . . . . All Jewish children were slated for murder. . .

> . . After the middle of 1942, the Germans seemed more determined to do away with "useless" ghetto Jews—the old, the sick, and children. [The Germans] attacked Jewish women through their born and unborn children. . . . Discriminatory laws [were] designed to undermine motherhood, pregnancy, and child care. Disobeying any of these laws resulted in punishment, usually death. . . . Wartime ghettos in Eastern Europe were closed communities in which brutality and cruelty took unprecedented forms. (Tec 2-4)

On Christmas Eve of 1942, Sender and I went to the ghetto hospital, so I could deliver my baby. After I had the baby, the Nazis took him from me and tore him apart. I will never forget this night and what happened to my baby boy. It is especially difficult for me to talk about what happened to him.

Chapter Ten
Deportations

After our baby was murdered, Sam and I continued trying to survive in the ghetto. We lived together with my mother and father. I stayed home, but Sam went out of the ghetto to work as a tailor.

When Ghetto #1 was liquidated on September 23 and 24, 1943, we were rounded up and taken outside the ghetto to Rossa Square where the Nazis selected people for the labor camps in Estonia and Latvia or for Sobibor (or Treblinka) death camp. The children and women were separated from the men. Then the women were selected into two groups. Those whom the Nazis thought incapable of work were sent with the children to Sobibor. The men and women who could work were gathered together; these men and some of the women were sent to Estonia labor camps, but most of the women were sent to Latvian labor camps. (Arad 137)

I don't know exactly what happened to my mother. She was taken when they separated the younger from the older women. Some say she was in a group that went to Sobibor Death Camp; others, that she was in a group that was murdered at Ponary.

Sender's mother, Sima, and his two sisters had gone into hiding, so they were not deported. The rest of us—about 3,700—were sent to slave labor camps in Estonia.

Sender and I were separated. He was sent to one slave labor camp in Estonia; I was sent to another. My father too was separated from us.

Chapter Eleven
Estonia

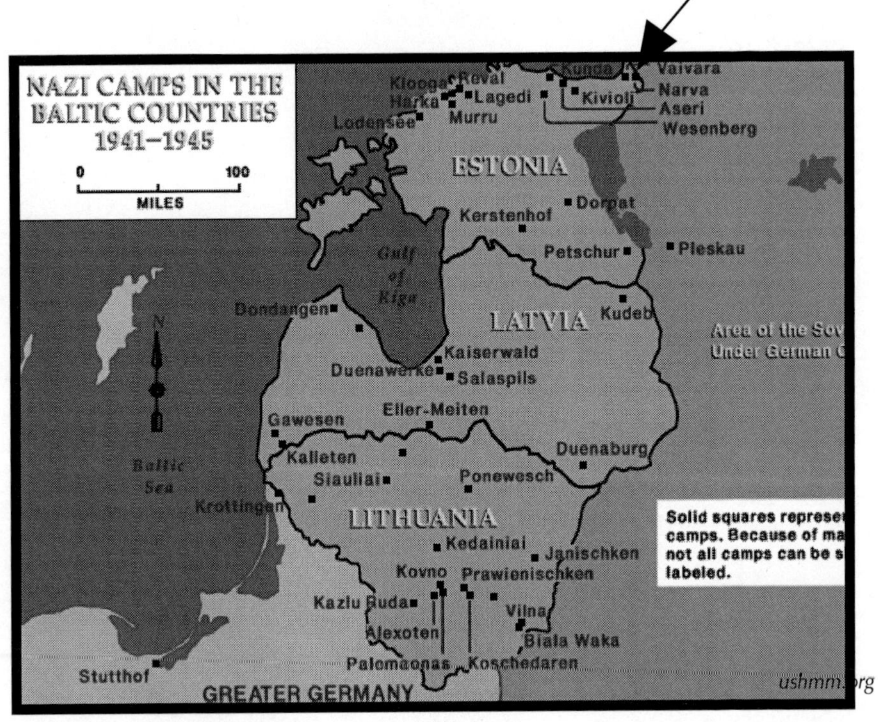
NAZI CAMPS IN THE BALTIC COUNTRIES 1941–1945
0
100
MILES
Klooga
Reval
Harka
Lagedi
Lodensee
Murru
Kunda
Kivioli
Vaivara
Narva
Aseri
Wesenberg
ESTONIA
Dorpat
Kerstenhof
Petschur
Pleskau
Gulf of Riga
Dondangen
LATVIA
Kudeb
Area of the Sov
Under German C
Kaiserwald
Duenawerke
Salaspils
Eller-Meiten
Gawesen
Kalleten
Duenaburg
Baltic Sea
Siauliai
Ponewesch
Krottingen
LITHUANIA
Kedainiai
Janischken
Kovno
Prawienischken
Solid squares represe
camps. Because of ma
not all camps can be s
labeled.
Kazlu Ruda
Vilna
Alexoten
Biala Waka
Palomaonas
Koschedaren
Stutthof
GREATER GERMANY
ushmm.org

Estonia's history during World War II resembled Vilna's:

> Estonia, the northernmost and smallest of the Baltic States, was initially occupied, as was Vilna, by the Soviet Red Army, as a result of the Non-aggression Treaty between the Germany Third Reich and the Soviet Union (see note 5). Although officially labeled a "non-aggression treaty," the pact included a secret protocol, in which the independent countries of Finland, Estonia, Latvia, Lithuania, Poland, and Romania were divided between Germany and the Soviet Union. (ushmm.org)
>
> The peaceful and active life of the small Estonian Jewish community, about 4500 in 1939, came to an abrupt halt in 1940 with the Soviet occupation of Estonia. Cultural autonomy, in addition to all of its institutions, was destroyed in July 1940. In July and August of the same year all organizations, associations, societies, and corporations were closed. A large group of Jews (about 400) were deported to Siberia on June 14,1941. (ushmm.org)
>
> By late autumn of 1941, the Germans had taken over all of Estonia, until then occupied by the Soviet Red Army. Estonia was then a part of the *Reichskommissariat Ostland*, a German civilian administration, including the Baltic States and Belarus.
>
> According to Weiss-Wendt, because of the

perception that the Estonian Jews had cooperated with the Soviets, Estonian Jews under German occupation became "the focus of accentuated hostile attitudes among the [non-Jewish] Estonians," as we saw with the Lithuanian non-Jews in Vilna. Some of these non-Jewish Estonians collaborated, assisting the Nazis and themselves actively participating in the Holocaust in Estonia (321).

"From early on, the Germans subjected Estonian Jews to harsh measures including confiscation of property and forcing them to wear yellow badges identifying them as Jews. These measures were only temporary as the Nazis prepared to murder all Estonian Jews. German SS and police units, together with Estonian auxiliaries, massacred the Jews of Estonia by the end of 1941. No ghettos were created in Estonia during the German occupation." (ushmm.org)

About 500 Jews managed to escape to Russia and were exiled to Siberia. (simonweisenthalcenter.org)

After the war, a number of Jews who had previously fled to the Soviet Union returned to Soviet-occupied Estonia. There was, however, no rebirth of Jewish cultural life. Communist Party policies were hostile to Jews and were implemented as part of an Anti-Zionism campaign. Hence, in addition to physical destruction, the Jews in Estonia met cultural catastrophe.

The restoration of Estonian independence in 1991

brought about numerous political, economic, and social changes. The Jews living in Estonia could now defend their rights as a national minority. The Jewish Community was re-established in 1992, and its charter was approved on April 11, 1992.

In July 2005, Estonia unveiled a memorial stone in the former concentration camp in Klooga, one of the Vaivara camps. Some 1,500 Estonian Jews died in the Vaivara camps, and an estimated 10,000 Jews from other countries such as Poland, were killed in Estonia after having been deported to camps there from elsewhere in Eastern Europe.

On May 2007 the community celebrated the opening of its first synagogue since the country's Jewish community was destroyed in the Holocaust. (jewishvirtuallibrary.org)

Chapter Twelve
Vaivara

Upon arrival in Estonia, I discovered the destination of the train that had deported us. We were sent, as were tens of thousands of Jews from other countries, to forced labor camps in Estonia as part of the Nazi resettlement plan. The main holding camp was Vaivara, a concentration and transit camp in northeast Estonia, located near the Soviet/Estonian border (see map in the previous chapter). [13]

From August 1943 until February 1944, Vaivara was the central camp of about twenty labor camps established throughout Estonia, including Ereda, Goldfilz, Kalevi Liiva, Kivioli I and II, Klooga, Narva, and Vivikond. Some twenty thousand Jews from the ghettos of Vilna and Kovno in Lithuania [including Ida, Ida's father, and Sender], passed through these camps. The administrative staff was made up of SS Death-Head Units, headed by SS Hans Aumeier, who had previously served at Auschwitz, Dachau, and Buchenwald. [14] Vaivara was guarded by an Estonian SS unit.

Prisoners, many of them Jewish, were forced to build military defenses for the German army, mine shale oil, dig antitank ditches, quarry large stones, and fell trees in forest and swamp areas. (motlc.org)

In 1943, I arrived in Estonia and was sent to Vaivara, a German SS-run concentration camp. My father and Sender had also been deported, but they were not deported in the same cattle car as I. We had arrived from Vilna after a journey of several days, a journey that seemed much longer because of the over-crowded cars, the stench, and the lack of water.

At Vaivara, the cattle cars were unloaded, and we lined up. I saw that the camp was surrounded by barbed wire as well as by a kind of moat—a ditch full of water encircled the camp. I looked for Sender and my father among the others. However, I did not see them then. I felt very much alone.

Chapter Thirteen
Life in Vaivara

After selection in Vaivara, the women who had been selected for work were taken to a building, stripped, and put on tables. They shaved us all over. Some young girls cried and cried. I said to them, in Yiddish, "Don't cry! As long as you have a head, you'll have hair. Don't give them the satisfaction of seeing you crying." At this time they gave me a striped uniform and my number, 1055 or 1059, on a *shmatteh* (Yiddish: piece of cloth) that I pinned to my clothing.

They then put us in wooden huts with thin walls that were not insulated against the heat and cold. These huts, the so-called barracks, were divided into three sections with seventy or eighty prisoners in each section—each hut was very over-crowded. In my barrack, there was a small stove but it didn't heat well; therefore, I was very cold—freezing. We slept in three-tiered bunk beds, ten in a row. I wore a blanket in the morning to wrap around me when I went to roll call in the brutally cold early morning air.

Each day we had roll call at 5:00 AM. We waited a long time while they counted us before we could go to work. In the morning we had a watery drink they called coffee. In the afternoon we were given watery soup to drink and a small piece of moldy bread to eat. I was desperately hungry. I "organized" potatoes from the fields so I wouldn't starve. [15] I hid them in my clothing when I returned to the camp. I used to roast them in the small stove in our barrack.

Water was scarce. There were no washing facilities. In the beginning there were just holes to be used as toilets. Later there were boards with holes in them—inadequate because there were many prisoners. I washed in snow or with a little of the drinking water that they gave us. I tried to keep myself clean because I was afraid that I would catch diseases if I didn't.

Despite my efforts at cleanliness, I caught typhus. Many people in Vaivara died from typhus carried by lice. [16] These were big lice—all over everyone, thousands of them.[17] I was very ill, but some kind person in my barrack helped me, giving me warm water to drink. Therefore, somehow I survived this deadly disease. I also survived a big selection in which three hundred people who had typhus were taken away to be murdered.

Later there were selections every two weeks, when about 500 prisoners were murdered—often taken to the forest and shot by the German or Estonian SS.

Their bodies were carried away and burned by Jewish men, *Sonderkommandos* (special *Kommando* or work duty, dealing with corpses). They were forced to do this. Most *Sonderkommando* only lasted three or four months, and then they were killed, so they would not tell about what they had seen.

The Germans forced me to do many different kinds of work: I worked in the woods, chopping wood; I cleaned police stations for the Germans; and I worked on the railroad, laying down new railroad ties. All of this was back-breaking work, especially to malnourished people; the SS wanted to work us to death.

We were guarded by a few older German civilians, who could speak Polish. They were good to us, sometimes giving us salt or whatever food they could hide for us.

In July and August of 1944 the Soviet Army advanced north through Nazi-occupied Estonia toward Vaivara.

Chapter Fourteen
My Father and My Husband

I saw neither my father nor my husband in Vaivara Concentration Camp. However, over a year after my arrival in Vaivara, when I was sent to a sub camp to work, I saw my father. He was working at different jobs, in the woods or on the railroad. I was so happy to see him and to know that he was still alive. I had hope that Sender may also have survived. Then, I heard, they had taken my father away to the woods and murdered him. They gave me his shoes to hurt me so that I would know he was dead. I was terribly upset.

I never saw Sender in Vaivara.

Unknown to Ida, while Ida was in Vaivara, Sender was in another section of the camp. His job was repairing German uniforms. One day he tried to smuggle in a loaf of bread that he had gotten outside the camp—whether this was for Ida or someone else is not known. A guard caught him and beat him over his head and he lost his hearing in one ear for the rest of his life. (He never had a hearing aid; as his son speculates, perhaps the reason he did not wear a hearing aid was vanity, or perhaps a hearing aid would not have helped, or perhaps he wanted to remember what had happened.)

Shortly after this beating, Sender escaped to the Rudnicki (Rudninkai) Forest and joined the partisans. In the opening scene from the film Partisans of Vilna, *there is a still shot of a group of eight or nine—Sender is one of them.* [18] (See the Photograph section.)

The Vilna partisan group was supported by the White Russians (Belarusians), who supplied them with arms and ammunition.

Chapter Fifteen
Death March

Ahead of the advancing Soviet army, the SS began to evacuate Vaivara Concentration Camp and its sub-camps in late August 1944. In Western Europe, the Allied armies began liberating other concentration camps in April of 1945.

> Near the end of World War II in 1944 and 1945, when Germany's military force was collapsing, the Allied armies closed in on the Nazi concentration camps. The Soviets approached from the east, and the British, French, and Americans from the west. The Germans began frantically to move the prisoners out of the camps near the front and took them to be used as forced laborers in camps inside Germany. Prisoners were first taken by train and then by foot on "death marches," as they became known. Prisoners were forced to march long distances in bitter cold, with little or no food, water, or rest. Those who could not keep up were shot. . . . .
>
> The evacuations of the concentration camps had three purposes:

(1) SS authorities did not want prisoners to fall into enemy hands alive to tell their stories to Allied and Soviet liberators.

(2) The SS thought they needed prisoners to maintain production of armaments, whenever possible.

(3) Some SS leaders, including Himmler, believed irrationally that they could use Jewish concentration camp prisoners as hostages to bargain for a separate peace in the west that would guarantee the survival of the Nazi regime. (ushmm.org)

Many prisoners from Vaivara were sent west by the sea to Stutthof Concentration Camp, a camp about 22 miles east of Danzig (Gdansk). Others were sent on death marches along the Baltic coast. [19]

I was sent on a death march to the south, wearing wooden clogs, which were almost impossible to walk in. The weather was already quite frigid. I was freezing. I said to the Germans walking with us, "Kill me here." But they didn't. Other women on the death march encouraged me, coaxing me, "Come with us. We'll help each other." So they *shlepped* (Yiddish: pulled along) me with them.

One night we stopped at a cement factory to rest. People from the village came to look at us. They didn't know what was going on. In Polish I said to them, "I am a Jew." They may already have known this because the SS had painted a red cross on the back of my coat—to mark me as a Jew. In addition, I wore my number on a *shmatteh* pinned to my coat. One Pole said to me, "I live across the road. I'll walk across. You follow me because, otherwise, they will kill you tomorrow." Four of us escaped like that. *(Two of us are still alive.)*

I stayed with these Poles for six weeks. They were refugees from other areas of Poland, sent by the Germans to do slave labor. These kind Poles gave me food. In the daytime they hid me and watched for the Germans. At night I slept in a bed with pillows! Other places in the village were hiding the other girls.

When the Germans left the area, the Russians, advancing from the east, arrived near the cement factory. So I was liberated and had to then think what I would do. I decided to go back to Vilna to try to find Sender. I met a Polish woman, also a refugee, who helped me because I was weak and malnourished. She took me on a train. I got off at a small train station, at a suburb to the west of Vilna. When I got off the train and walked into the station, I met this Holocaust survivor group there. I knew some of the people in this group. They were trying to decide where they would go.

I stayed in this village with the other survivors for a while. Then I began walking east towards Vilna to see if I could find anyone alive. I still had a little hope that Sender had survived—but only a glimmer of hope.

Chapter Sixteen
Return to Vilna

On my way back to Vilna, I stopped at a Jewish Community Center on the outskirts of the city and they told me, "There is nobody in Vilna. No Jews are there." They asked me if I thought my husband, Sender, was alive. I said, "No. He was in the same concentration camp in Estonia but in a different section. I never saw him. But I have to be sure that he did not survive."

Therefore, I continued walking toward Vilna to discover for myself his fate. On the road I saw Jewish people leaving Vilna. They asked me, "Why are you going there? No one is left."

Yet I met Sender, my husband, as we were both going toward Vilna.

Sender had been a partisan. At the time we met he was going from town to town trying to find out who was still alive. He had heard that Jewish women were staying in a community center nearby. He looked in, looking for me. I wasn't there, but some people from Vilna recognized him and told him, "Ida is here. You wait here and we will go to find her."

People ran up to me and told me that Sender was with them. They said, "Sender is here. We'll take you to him."

So Sender and I were reunited. Amazing! So many people displaced by the war—Poles, Russians, Lithuanians, Estonians, Germans—and I found Sender!

Sender had been back to Vilna. He had learned that his mother, Sima, had been liberated by the Soviet Army when Vilna was liberated on July 13, 1944. However, when she was looking for the rest of her family, she and her two daughters, who had been in hiding with her, were killed by Polish antisemites. [20]

Sender's parents had had twelve children: nine boys and three girls. Three brothers, including Sender, and one sister survived—one brother went to Israel and then immigrated to Canada, and another brother immigrated to the United States and had a farm in New Jersey. The sister who survived had escaped to Russia and then immigrated to the United States in the 1960s.

When Sender went back to our home, the Poles whom Sender saw near our home told him that they would have him arrested if he didn't leave. "In postwar Poland, there were a number of pogroms (violent anti-Jewish riots). The largest of these occurred in the town of Kielce in 1946 when Polish rioters killed at least 42 Jews and beat many others." (ushmm.org)

Because of the anti-Semitism and our terrible memories of lost family members, especially of our baby son, we didn't want to stay in Vilna long. Moreover, as the Soviets had incorporated Vilna into the Soviet Union as the capital of the Lithuanian SSR in 1944, large numbers of Polish were being expelled to Poland.

With this dangerous political situation, we decided to leave Vilna and make a living somewhere else. Therefore, we paid money to a private group to smuggle us across the border into Czechoslovakia, and then we went on from there by ourselves. We paid them with jewelry left from one of my sister-in-laws.

Very few Jews stayed in Vilna after World War II. Few Jews had survived the slave labor and death camps. Ninety percent of Vilna Jews were murdered.

> *Vilnius's Jewish population today is 6,000 (1997), about ten percent of what it once was. The entire country is home to only 7,500 Jews, some 200 of whom are Holocaust survivors. Most of the two hundred pre-war communities were decimated, entirely wiped off the map. Few people speak Yiddish anymore. The Jewish community publishes the* Jerusalem of Lithuania*—a four-language periodical in Yiddish, Lithuanian, English, and Russian, reporting the events in the life of the community with a special emphasis on the cultural aspects.*
>
> *Today, there remains one synagogue in Vilnius: The Choral Synagogue, built in a Moorish style and opened in September 1903, is the only active synagogue in Vilna.*
>
> *(jewishvirtuallibrary.org; bh.org.il)*

Chapter Seventeen
The Surviving Remnant

They were the survivors of the Holocaust, the remnants of their families, their culture, their faith. Displaced from everything, they organized under the Hebrew name, Sh'erit ha-Pletah, the surviving remnant.

–From Life Reborn, an exhibit of the USHMM

Sender and I were not the only displaced persons seeking a better and a safer life.

During World War II, seven to nine million people were displaced from their homes for various reasons. After the war most of these people wanted to return home. However, of those nine million, one and a half to two million displaced persons (DPs) refused to return to their homes, fearing economic and social repercussions, or even annihilation. About ten percent of these people were Jewish. (fcit.usf.edu)

Many DPs were from other countries in Europe or from the Soviet Union. Some were even returning from countries as far away as China and Japan.

The majority of the displaced had been incarcerated in Nazi concentration camps, slave labor camps, and prisoner-of-war camps liberated by the Allied armies as these armies fought their way through German-occupied territory in the east and west.

After they were liberated, these displaced people, recovering from hardship, neglect, abuse, torture, and often attempted murder, found themselves in unfamiliar places trying to decide what they should do next. Their immediate concerns were food, shelter, and basic health care. Most DPs had survived on starvation diets—less than 1,000 calories a day.

Sanitary conditions had been deplorable, and they had had minimal or no medical care. As a result, they suffered from malnutrition, a variety of diseases, and were often unclean and lice-ridden. Because their immune systems had been compromised, they were prone to illness.

In addition, most of the refugees suffered from psychological difficulties. They were often distrustful and apprehensive around authorities, and many were depressed and traumatized.

After satisfying their essential needs, displaced persons were anxious to be reunited with families. Efforts to identify survivors were formalized through the United Nations Relief and Rehabilitation Administration (UNRRA)'s [21] Central Tracking Bureau and the facilities of the International Red Cross. These organizations collected the names of over one million survivors in the post-war period.

> The Allies set up DP camps in Western Europe, camps usually administered by American, British, and French military. Displaced persons often moved from camp to camp, looking for family, countrymen, or better food, accommodations, etc. Over time, ethnic and religious groups concentrated in certain camps. (ushmm.org)

"The Jewish DPs (known as the *Sh'erit ha-Pletah*—the "Surviving Remnant") became long-term wards of UNRRA and the occupying forces. By late 1945, camp operations were administered entirely by UNRRA and other voluntary agencies, most notably the American Jewish Joint Distribution Committee (Joint).[22] Early in 1946 those agencies and the Allied armies recognized a new de facto authority—the organized Jewish DPs themselves." (ushmm.org)

One question that faced the Western world was, "Who will offer homes to these displaced people?" (fcit.usf.edu)

> As a result of the 1948 and 1950 DP Acts, under the auspices of President Harry Truman, and the establishment of the state of Israel in 1948, Jewish DPs emigrated *en masse* from Europe, settling mainly in Israel and the United States—80,000 in the United States, about 136,000 in Israel, and another 20,000 in other nations, including Canada and South Africa. By 1952 only one DP camp was still open. (ushmm.org)

Chapter Eighteen
Gailingen DP Camp

After Sender and I left the Vilna area in 1946, we eventually came to Gailingen, a small German town located on the northern bank of the Rhine River just across from Switzerland and close to Lake Constance.[23] Gailingen had had one of the largest Jewish communities in the south of Germany. Jews had lived there in harmony with their non-Jewish neighbors until the rise of Hitler, when the community had been destroyed—first deported to France and then to Auschwitz-Birkenau Concentration Camp in Poland.

In 1946, forty families of Holocaust survivors lived in Gailingen in an abandoned retirement home—then called the *Friedrichsheim* Senior Citizen Home (see Photograph section). There we ate twice a day. A German woman cooked for our community and we ate in a communal kitchen.

Most people survived by buying and selling on the black market. They sold watches, chocolate, and stockings—all items that were scarce after the war.

There were many weddings and many births in the European DP camps. Ours was no exception. On September 5, 1946, our son, Leon (now Lee) was born in this camp. We had a Greek (or perhaps she was Italian) girl who watched Lee. She had come looking for work because the economic situation in her country was dire. She needed a job to support herself, and we hired her.

After World War II, both Italy's and Greece's economies were shattered. Italy was a disaster: Cities were ruined. Railroads destroyed. The Italian overseas empire was stripped. Their navy had been lost. The currency was debased. The people were impoverished. (answers.com) Many, such as Lee's "nanny," left their countries to seek work elsewhere.

Italy's economy did not begin to grow again until 1948. "The most significant contributory factor to this growth was the Marshall Plan (1948–51), a US-sponsored program to regenerate the postwar economies of Western Europe" (Britannica.com).

In Greece the situation was equally, if not more disastrous. "World War II left Greece in a desperate economic situation. Three occupying forces (Germany, Italy, Bulgaria) had divided the country, destroyed its infrastructure and depressed the already low living standards of the Greek people." (Psalidopoulos 1)

After liberation, Greece was plagued by hyperinflation. This situation was complicated by substantial losses in agriculture, heavy damage to industrial and shipping capital, and acerbated by a lack of raw materials and damaged transport and communications facilities. Then came the Truman Doctrine and with it the American commitment to support democracy in Greece, followed in 1947 by the Marshall Plan, which, as in Italy, started the Greek economy growing (Psalidopoulos 1-2).

Chapter Nineteen
Immigration

In 1949, Sender and I decided to immigrate to the United States. However, we needed an affidavit from the United States saying that someone would sponsor us, so we would not be a burden on the US. Older people, former neighbors from Vilna—Mayer Judalevitz and his wife—who knew my husband, sent us this affidavit. They had a farm in Mays Landing, New Jersey.

On September 24 or 25, 1949, the ship sailed from Danzig (present day Gdansk), Poland, to Copenhagen, Denmark, to the United States. Sender, Lee, three years old and talking, and I docked in Boston, but after a few days we went to Brooklyn. We went to Brooklyn because the Trockis were there. They had known us in Vilna. I had gone to school with Jack Trocki. He helped a lot of people.

Chapter Twenty
The Farm in Vineland

After a brief time in Brooklyn, in 1949, we went to Mays Landing, New Jersey. We chose this area for two reasons. First, the American Jewish Joint Distribution Committee (Joint—see note 22) had said, "New Jersey is the place for you. All you need to do is work and collect eggs. You don't need to know the language." The second reason was that we knew people in South Jersey—the Judalevitz couple.

Mayer Judalevitz and his wife, who were real estate brokers, helped us to find a farm. We bought a five-acre chicken farm in East Vineland, on Tuckahoe Road.

There was a bungalow with a coal stove and some chicken coops. While my husband worked as a tailor in a clothing factory in Hammonton, I took care of the chickens—a lot of work, 24 hours a day, seven days a week. We bought a bunch of chickens—baby chicks, because we wanted to raise them and then sell eggs. However, this first batch became sick with cholera. The doctor said, "Get rid of them." So we had no eggs from that flock. The chickens were rough too; they often cut me with their beaks. Despite problems, eventually we had 10,000 chickens.

On July 27, 1955, while we were on the farm, we became citizens (see Photograph section). Sender became Sam, and Leon became Lee—more American-sounding names. Our last name was changed from Fajnberg to Feinberg, as part of the Naturalization process.

Lee grew up on the farm. He helped in the coops; he worked hard. He went to Vineland Elementary School and then graduated from Vineland High School in 1964. Lee celebrated his *Bar Mitzvah* in Atlantic City at the famous Teplitsky Hotel and Restaurant on the Broadwalk, where they served kosher-style food.[24] He was an excellent student and went on to Drexel University in Philadelphia, Pennsylvania, where he took out loans and paid for college himself. Sam and I couldn't afford to pay for his college. We were proud of how hard he worked to get a college education and his engineering degree.

We had friends among the Holocaust survivors who had also settled in the area. There were none within walking distance, but some lived in nearby Vineland.

On October 15, 1954, during Hurricane Hazel, which was, at that time, the worst hurricane of the twentieth-century as well as the only recorded Category 4 hurricane to make landfall as far north as North Carolina, we lost everything—the bungalow, chicken coops, and chickens. Hazel's winds gusted over 100 miles per hour and the hurricane hit during the highest lunar tide of the year (weather.net). Since Hazel, I can't stand the sound of the wind. *When I hear it now, I shut my blinds to block the sight and sound of the wind.*

After Hurricane Hazel, we rebuilt the farm and for another eight years we worked the farm. Sam did both—his tailoring and the farming. We rented a place near Cherry Hill in Haddonfield where Sam had his tailoring business.

Eventually, in 1964, we got rid of everything, the chickens and the farm. We almost gave the farm away at $12,000. We sold it to a Russian refugee couple that my son knew. The woman had gone to high school with my son. They came to look at the place and Sam felt sorry for them and gave them a bargain.

Chapter Twenty-One
Maple Shade

After we left the farm in 1964, Sam continued with his tailoring work. I continued to help out. We rented an apartment in Maple Shade, New Jersey, where we lived until I moved to Ventnor, and everyday I would go to work with Sam. Every morning I would give him juice. Then at the shop in Haddonfield we would eat bagels and drink some coffee.

One time I had shingles and I was in terrible pain.[25] But I still went with my husband. I sat in a recliner in the back. The accountant who was doing our income tax told me to go to the doctor. The doctor gave me at least six needles, but I was still in pain. A customer noticed that I was grimacing in pain and asked me what was wrong. When I told him about the shingles, he told me to put wet cloths on my chest. This did help with the pain.

One day Sam asked me, "Why do you come to work with me every day, even when you are ill with shingles?" I told him that I liked to be together with him. Who knows what would happen? If something did, we would be together.

In 1997, my husband decided to retire. However, not long

after he retired, Sam complained of feeling sick and being cold all the time. The doctor came to the house, but after examining my husband, he sent Sam immediately to the hospital. My husband asked the doctor, "How long do I have to live?" The doctor replied, "Ninety days, Sam."

Sam had lung cancer. He lived exactly ninety days. Sam died late in 1997. Sam was born on the first candle of Chanukah and died on the last candle of Chanukah.

Chapter Twenty-Two
Epilogue

When Sam died in December 1997, I again felt very alone. After a time, my son, Lee, brought me to Atlantic City, New Jersey, to look at a number of condominiums. When he brought me to my condominium, I liked it right away. I liked the open space with the kitchen, dining room, and living area not in separate rooms. I moved in during the spring of 1998. I have been living there since then.

Lee suggested I get rid of most of my old furniture, so I could make a new start. My wonderful daughter-in-law, Bonnie, helped me to furnish and decorate the condominium. I have a beautiful view of the beach and the ocean.

My son, Lee, who had graduated Drexel University in Philadelphia with an engineering degree, now works in the financial services industry for UBS. Lee has two children—my grandchildren—David, born in 1978, a researcher at Goldman Sachs, who is married to Katie, and Jonathan, born in 1986, who is studying at Duke University in North Carolina, majoring in political science and women studies.

I am proud of all of them. I love them and they love me. My son calls me every day at 3:00 PM, and my grandchildren call me often. They help to make my life worthwhile. Their love makes the sun shine for me again. They are my triumph! Because of them, after the night of the Holocaust, the dawn and the sun did come again.

Works Cited

Websites:

bh.org.il
deathcamps.org
fcit.usf.edu
jewishvirtuallibrary.org
motlc.learningcenter.wiesenthal.org
neris.mii.it
nizkor.org (Eichmann Trial transcripts)
ushmm.org
weather.net

Maps:

cia.gov
deathcamps.org
greenwichmeantime.com
ushmm.org

Books and Articles:

Arad, Yitzhak. *Belzec, Sobibor, Treblinka: The Operation Reinhard Death Camps*. Bloomington: Indiana UP, 1999. 137.

Beinfeld, Solon. "Health Care in the Vilna Ghetto." *Holocaust and Genocide Studies* 12.1 (1998): 66-98.

Matthüs, Jürgen. "Key Aspects of German Anti-Jewish Policy." *Lithuania and the Jews—The Holocaust Chapter*. Washington, DC: USHMM, 2005. 24-38.

Psalidopoulos, Michael. "Economic Thought and Greek Post-World War II Reconstruction, 1944-1953." <www.econ.uoa.gr>.

Ran, Leyzer. *The Jerusalem of Lithuania*. Egg Harbor City, NJ : Laureate P, 1974.

Tec, Nechama. *Jewish Children: Between Protectors and Murderers*. Washington, DC: USHMM, 2005.

Venclova, Tomas. "The End of the World in Vilna." Rev. of *From That Place and Time a Memoir, 1938-1947*. By Lucy S. Dawidowicz. *New York Times*. July 23, 1989. New York Times.com.

Weiss-Wendt, Anton. "The Soviet Occupation of Estonia in 1940-41 and the Jews." *Holocaust and Genocide Studies* 12.2 (1998): 308-25.

Ida (R) and her friend Betty (L), now Mrs. Betty Katz—before the Holocaust

Sender, before the Holocaust

A group of the partisans of Vilna: Sender is in the second row, his head down, behind the partisan in the cap with the rifle. From the back cover of the DVD The Partisans of Vilna.

THE UNITED STATES OF AMERICA

ORIGINAL
TO BE GIVEN TO
THE PERSON NATURALIZED

No. 7117263

CERTIFICATE OF NATURALIZATION

Petition No. 9711

Personal description of holder as of date of naturalization: Date of birth September 15, 1920 sex Female complexion Fair color of eyes Brown color of hair Brown height 5 feet 2 inches weight 120 pounds; visible distinctive marks None
Marital status Married former nationality Stateless last of Poland
I certify that the description above given is true, and that the photograph affixed hereto is a likeness of me.

Sign here

x Ida Feinberg
(Complete and true signature of holder)

Ida Feinberg
seal

State of New Jersey
County of Atlantic } ss:

Be it known, that at a term of the Atlantic County Court of Atlantic County, New Jersey held pursuant to law at Mays Landing, New Jersey on July 27th, 1955 the Court having found that Ida Feinberg then residing at R.D.#5, Tuckahoe Rd., Buena, East Vineland, N.J. intends to reside permanently in the United States (when so required by the Naturalization Laws of the United States), had in all other respects complied with the applicable provisions of such naturalization laws, and was entitled to be admitted to citizenship, thereupon ordered that such person be and (s)he was admitted as a citizen of the United States of America.

In testimony whereof the seal of the court is hereunto affixed this 27th day of July in the year of our Lord nineteen hundred and Fifty-five and of our Independence the one hundred and Eightieth

W. A. Blair
Clerk of the Atlantic County Court.

By ______ Deputy Clerk.

It is a violation of the U.S. Code (and punishable as such) to copy, print, photograph, or otherwise illegally use this certificate.

DEPARTMENT OF JUSTICE

Ida's naturalization document for citizenship. Ryan, this document should be moved

Jonathan, Ida, David, Lee, and Bonnie

Ida, 2007. *Photo credit Sheila Nuss.*

Endnotes

[1] **But if the dawn and sun come too late for us**. This is a variation of the title of Ida's memoir, *If the Dawn is Late in Coming*, from the "Partisan's Song."

[2] **Partisan's Song** "Of all the songs of all the ghettos, the one which spread like wildfire, was the 'Song of the Partisans' by Hirsh Glik, 'Zog nit keynmol az du geyst dem letstn vet'('Never Say that You Are Trodding the Final Path'). It used a tune by the Soviet brothers Pokras, and it became the official resistance hymn of all the Eastern European partisan brigades. It was translated into Hebrew, Polish, Russian, Spanish, Romanian, Dutch, and English. It was well known in all the concentration camps." *—www.fcit.usf.edu/HOLOCAUST/arts/musVicti*

[3] **Vilna**

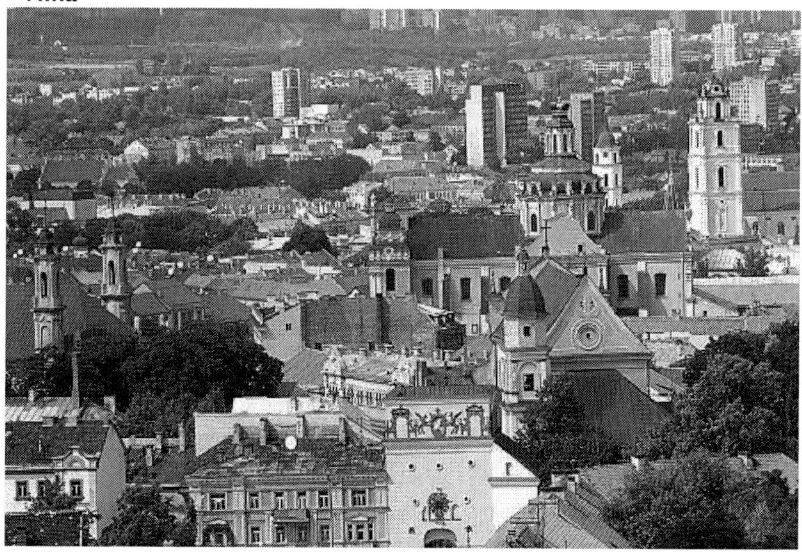

Vilna 1941-1943

"Poland and Lithuania both claimed Vilna (Vilnius) after World War I. Polish forces occupied Vilna in 1920, and before the outbreak of World War II, the city of Vilna was part of northeastern Poland. Under the terms of the German-Soviet Pact, Vilna, along with the rest of Eastern Poland, was occupied by Soviet forces in late September 1939. In October 1939, the Soviet Union transferred the Vilna region to Lithuania. However, Soviet forces occupied Lithuania in June 1940 and in August 1940 incorporated Vilna, along with the rest of Lithuania, into the Soviet Union. On June 22, 1941, Germany attacked Soviet forces in Eastern Europe. The German army occupied Vilna on June 24, 1941, the third day after the invasion.

The Germans established two ghettos—ghetto #1 and ghetto #2—in Vilna in early September 1941. Jews considered incapable of work were concentrated in ghetto #2. In October 1941, German *Einsatzgruppen* (mobile killing squads) detachments and Lithuanian auxiliaries destroyed ghetto #2, killing the ghetto population in Ponary, a wooded area about eight miles southwest of Vilna.

Lukiszki Prison served as a collection center for Jews who were to be taken to Ponary and shot. By the end of 1941, the *Einsatzgruppen* had killed about 40,000 Jews in Ponary.

The Jews in ghetto #1 were forced to work in factories or in construction projects outside the ghetto. Some Jews were sent to labor camps in the Vilna region. In periodic killing operations, most of the ghetto's inhabitants were massacred at Ponary. From the spring of 1942 until the spring of 1943, there were no mass killing operations in Vilna. The Germans renewed the killings during the final liquidation of ghetto #1 in late September 1943. Children, the elderly, and the sick were sent to the Sobibor extermination camp or were shot at Ponary. The surviving men were sent to labor camps in Estonia, while the women were sent to labor camps in Latvia.

The Vilna ghetto had a significant Jewish resistance movement. A group of Jewish partisans known as the United Partisan Organization *(Fareynegte Partizaner Organizatsye;* FPO) was formed in 1942 and operated within the ghetto. The resistance created hiding places for weapons and prepared to fight the Germans. In early September 1943, realizing that the Germans intended the final destruction of the ghetto, resistance members skirmished with the Germans, who had entered the ghetto to begin the deportations. The Jewish council, however, agreed to cooperate in the deportations of Jews from the ghetto, hoping to minimize bloodshed. Consequently, the FPO decided to flee to the nearby forests to fight the Germans. Some ghetto fighters escaped the final destruction of the ghetto, leaving through the sewers to join partisans in the Rudninkai (Rudnicki) and Naroch forests outside the city.

In September 1943, in an attempt to destroy the evidence of the killing of Jews at Ponary, the Germans forced detachments of Jewish laborers to open the mass graves and burn the corpses. Jews from nearby labor camps continued to be killed at Ponary. During the German occupation, tens of thousands of Jews from Vilna and the surrounding area, as well as Soviet prisoners of war and others suspected of opposing the Germans, were massacred at Ponary.

The Soviet army liberated Vilna in July 1944." *–rtrfoundation.org*

[4] ***Numerus Clausus***, "a Latin term meaning a restricted number, refers to the practice of setting a quota for the number of persons of some category—usually Jews—who will be admitted to an educational institution, most often a university. This type of discrimination was normal in Czarist Russia. After World War I, the use of *Numerus Clausus* was formalized in Hungary, where the number of Jews who could be admitted to the universities was officially designated as no more than five percent of the total enrollment. It became a common practice at universities in other European countries as well; in Poland, the quota for Jewish admissions was ten percent.

Beginning in the 1920's a similar practice allowed unofficial, but widely observed quotas on Jewish enrollment at universities in the United States, particularly at the more prestigious schools in the northeastern states. These were the schools to which the children of recent Jewish immigrants were most likely to seek admission.

In recent years several major American universities in the western states have been investigated for following a similar policy to restrict the number of Asian student admissions. —www.humboldt.edu

Use of *Numerus Clausus* pre-World War I

Before the Second World War, the limitations in eastern European countries were usually based on the religion of the student, in particular limiting the number of students of Jewish origin.

This limitation took the form of total prohibition of Jewish students, or of limiting the number of Jewish students, so that their share in the student population would not be larger than their share in the general population (Jewish quota). It was introduced with a view to balancing the chances for an education among ethnic groups.

The *Numerus Clausus* policies affected a limited number of people, since the number of university students before World War II was very small.

Jews who wanted a university education used various ways to handle this obstacle: bribing the authorities, changing their religion, or traveling to countries without such limitations. In Hungary, for example, 5,000 Jewish youngsters (including Edward Teller [Father of the Hydrogen Bomb]) left the country after the introduction of the *Numerus Clausus*.

The Hungarian *Numerus Clausus* was introduced in 1920, as the first Anti-Jewish Act of twentieth century Europe in response to the recently overthrown communist and Jewish dominated regime of Bela Kun. Eighty percent of the top 30 commissars in the regime had been Jewish. Its aim was to restrict the number of Jews to 6%, same as the population rate; the rate of Jewish students was 25-40% in the 1910s in different faculties. In 1928—because of the pressure of liberal capital and the League of Nations—a less-explicit version of the act was passed. In the period of 1938-1945 the anti-Jewish acts were revitalised.

<u>*Numerus Clausus* in Poland</u>

Poland tried to introduce a formal *Numerus Clausus* law in 1923, but faced objections from the League of Nations. However, a *Numerus Clausus* was unofficially introduced in 1937 by some universities and the share of Jewish students was limited to 10%, which was more or less the proportion of Jews in the population of Poland (compared to 20%-60% before regulation).

The *Numerus Clausus* caused many Jewish students to emigrate from Poland, and therefore saved their lives during the German Holocaust. The *Numerus Clausus* was introduced at the level of universities, which in those times didn't educate many students (several thousands at best). However, the introduction of the policy must have had immense influence on the level of the average student.

The official reason for the policy was that during the Russian Tsar's rule, Poles were discriminated against in the area of education. They were denied education in Polish, and the schools were badly funded in the countryside. The advocates of the solution pointed out that the limit would balance the chance to enter university of all nationalities in Poland.

The other reason given by the supporters of the idea was that it was an attempt to equalize the chances of children from countryside families who had very limited access to education compared to the chances of the children of Jewish families living in the towns and cities. Nevertheless, the Polish intelligentsia of Jewish origins formed at least forty to fifty percent of the Polish educated class."

—*www.Humboldt.edu; answers.com*

[5] **Nazi-Soviet Pact (also called the Moscow Pact)** signed in Moscow on Thursday, August 24, 1939, by the Soviet foreign minister Vyacheslav Molotov and the German foreign minister Joachim von Ribbentrop. "The German-Russian Pact was signed in Moscow early this morning. It is to run for ten years, and the terms are as follows: Guided by the desire to strengthen the cause of peace between Germany and the Soviet Republics, and based on the fundamental stipulations of the neutrality agreement concluded in April, 1926, the German Government and the Soviet have come to the following agreement:

Article 1.

The two contracting Powers undertake to refrain from any act of force, any aggressive act, and any attacks against each other, or in conjunction with any other Powers." —century.guardian.co.uk

The Pact lasted until June 22, 1941 when Germany attacked the Soviet Union.

[6] ***Purim*** one of the most joyous holidays. It commemorates a time when the Jewish people living in Persia were saved from extermination.

"The story of *Purim* is told in the Biblical Book of Esther. The heroes of the story are Esther, a beautiful young Jewish woman living in Persia, and her cousin Mordecai, who raised her as if she were his daughter. Esther was taken to the house of Ahasuerus, King of Persia, to become part of his harem, and he loved her more than his other women and made her queen. But the king did not know that Esther was a Jew, because Mordecai told her not to reveal her nationality.

The villain of the story is Haman, an arrogant, egotistical advisor to the king. Haman hated Mordecai because Mordecai refused to bow down to Haman, so Haman plotted to destroy the Jewish people. In a speech that is all too familiar to Jews, Haman told the king, "There is a certain people scattered abroad and dispersed among the peoples in all the provinces of thy kingdom; and their laws are diverse from those of every people; neither keep they the king's laws; therefore it does not profit the king to suffer them." Esther 3:8. The king gave the fate of the Jewish people to Haman, to do as he pleased to them. Haman planned to exterminate all of the Jews.

Mordecai persuaded Esther to speak to the king on behalf of the Jewish people. This was a dangerous thing for Esther to do, because anyone who came into the king's presence without being summoned could be put to death, and she had not been summoned. Esther fasted for three days to prepare herself; then she went into the king. He welcomed her. Later, she told him of Haman's plot against her people. The Jewish people were saved, and Haman was hanged on the gallows that had been prepared for Mordecai.

Purim is celebrated on the 14th day of *Adar*, which is usually in March. The 14th of *Adar* is the day that Haman chose for the extermination of the Jews.

The word *"Purim"* means "lots" and refers to the lottery that Haman used to choose the date for the massacre.

The *Purim* holiday is preceded by a minor fast, the Fast of Esther, which commemorates Esther's three days of fasting in preparation for her meeting with the king.

The primary commandment related to *Purim* is to hear the reading of the book of Esther. The book of Esther is commonly known as the *Megillah*, which means scroll. Although there are five books of Jewish scripture that are properly referred to as *Megillahs* (Esther, Ruth, Ecclesiastes, Song of Songs, and Lamentations), this is the one people usually mean when the speak of The *Megillah*. It is customary to boo, hiss, stamp feet and rattle gragers (noisemakers) whenever the name of Haman is mentioned in the service. The purpose of this custom is to "blot out the name of Haman."

We are also commanded to eat, drink and be merry. According to the *Talmud*, a person is required to drink until he cannot tell the difference between "cursed be Haman" and "blessed be Mordecai," though opinions differ as to exactly how drunk that is.

In addition, we are commanded to send out gifts of food or drink, and to make gifts to charity. The sending of gifts of food and drink is referred to as *shalach manos* (lit. sending out portions). Among Ashkenazic Jews, a common treat at this time of year is *hamentaschen* (lit. Haman's pockets). These triangular fruit-filled cookies are supposed to represent Haman's three-cornered hat.

It is customary to hold carnival-like celebrations on *Purim*, to perform plays and parodies, and to hold beauty contests. I have heard that the usual prohibitions against cross-dressing are lifted during this holiday, but I am not certain about that. Americans sometimes refer to *Purim* as the Jewish Mardi Gras.

Work is permitted as usual on *Purim*, unless of course it falls on a Saturday." *—www.jewishvirtuallibrary.org*

[7] ***Chuppah*** "the marriage canopy under which the bride and groom stand during traditional Jewish wedding ceremonies. Often supported by four poles and decorated with flowers and fringes, the *Chuppah* is a symbol of the marriage chamber in which Jewish weddings originally took place.

Historically, Jewish weddings were comprised of two separate parts, a betrothal ceremony and a wedding ceremony, that took place about a year apart. The bride would live in the home of her parents following the betrothal until the marriage ceremony, which would take place in a room or tent that the groom had set up for her. Later in history, the two ceremonies were combined and the marriage ceremony started to be performed publicly. At this new ceremony, the *Chuppah*, the portable marriage canopy, was included as a symbol of the chamber in which the marriage originally took place.

Today, the *Chuppah* is seen as symbolizing the new home that the couple will build together and the protection that they will extend to each other. Open on four sides, it invites the community to share in the joy of the wedding. In some communities, the bride and groom stand under the *tallis* (prayer shawl) that the groom will wear during the morning prayers following the wedding; in others, special marriage canopies may be made and passed down as family heirlooms." *—jewishvirtuallibrary.org*

[8] **Ponary** a village ten kilometers from Vilna. Ironically it was famous for its beautiful landscape and was a place many went to enjoy their holidays. It was also the killing site of over 100,000 Jews, Poles, and Russians from Vilna and other nearby towns and villages. "Ponary was chosen for the mass-murder of Jews, Soviet POWs, and civilians because there were several large pits, dug there by the Soviets between 1940 and 1941, to serve as diesel or petrol supply storage resources for the Red Army.

Three units of *Einsatzkommando* (led by Martin Weiss and August Hering) were normally utilized: the first transported and guarded the victims who were brought in lorries, in railway cars, or on foot from Vilnius to Ponary. The second guarded the killing site; the third was responsible for providing the killing squads.

Groups of 100-1,000 Jews were brought from the city, made to undress, and then led, ten to twenty at a time, to the edge of the pit and shot. After the shooting was complete, the corpses were covered with sand, and the next group was summoned. Not all shots were fatal. Some Jews were just wounded. Thus some people were able to crawl out of the pit and return to Vilnius and its ghetto. . . . . Aware of the advancing Red Army, the Germans tried to destroy the evidence of the mass killings. Paul Blobel, who had previously commanded *Einsatzkommando* 4a, responsible for the murder of 33,771 Jews over two days in September 1941 at Babi Yar (outside Kiev), was ordered to perform this task. His *Sonderkommando* 1005 (code-name for this massive operation) arrived at Ponary at the end of September 1943. Between that time and April 1944, they exhumed and burned approximately 68,000 corpses at Ponary.

A *Sonderkommando* (70 Jews from the Kailis Forced Labor Camp in Vilnius, and 10 Soviet POWs) had to exhume and burn the corpses, supervised by 80 heavily armed guards." *–www.deathcamps.org*

[9] **SS and SD** The *Schutzstaffel* (German for "Protective Squadron"), abbreviated ᛋᛋ (Runic) or **SS** (Latin), was a large security and paramilitary organization of the National Socialist German Workers Party (Nazi Party) in Germany. "Under the leadership of Heinrich Himmler between 1929 and 1945, the SS grew from a small paramilitary formation to become one of the largest and most powerful organizations in Nazi Germany. The Nazis regarded the SS as an elite unit, the party's Praetorian Guard, with all SS personnel selected on the principles of racial purity and unconditional loyalty to the Nazi Party.

The **SD** was the intelligence service of the SS. Membership in the SD was voluntary, and it had a membership of about 3,000 in 1943-45. The SD was the intelligence service of the SS during the years preceding the accession of the Nazis to power, though it became a much more important organization promptly thereafter. The task of the SD, after it became the intelligence service for State and Party, was to obtain secret information concerning the actual and potential enemies of the Nazi leadership so that appropriate action could be taken to destroy or neutralize opposition. To accomplish this task, the SD created an organization of agents and informants operating out of various SD regional offices established throughout the Reich." —fas.org

[10] **Menstruation in Ghettos and Concentration Camps** Imprisonment in ghettos and concentration camps during the Holocaust resulted in enormous emotional and psychological changes in the survivors. "In addition, studies reveal abrupt changes in short-term menstrual function but little long-term physical damage to reproductive function.

The mean age of the survivors at the time of internment was 23.4 ± 8.0 years (95% CI 22.7–24.1). Amenorrhea occurred in 94.8% of the women during encampment (95% CI 92.7%–96.5%), with 82.4% experiencing cessation of menses immediately after internment (95% CI 76.9%–85.6%). Only 0.6% of women (95% CI 0.12%–1.63%) menstruated longer than 4 months after internment. After liberation, all but 8.9% of the women resumed menstruation within the first year (95% CI 88.4%–93.3%). Fecundity subsequent to liberation was not significantly affected by the imprisonment nor was there a significant increase in spontaneous abortion, ectopic pregnancies, stillbirths, or other pregnancy complications. Additionally, there was no evidence of impact on the subsequent frequency of gynecologic diseases or surgical procedures." – -*www.sciencedirect.com*

[11] Jacob Gens (1905-1943)

First, director of the Jewish Hospital, later Gens was commander of the Jewish police, and in this capacity he helped many Jews escape deportation to Ponary. In July 1942, he was made head of the *Judenrat*, initiating his "work for life" program; Gens believed the Jews would be productive and then the Germans would not liquidate the ghetto. Gens believed that the underground resistance endangered the ghetto's safety; therefore, he turned into the Germans the underground commander Wittenberg. During the *Aktionen* in August and September of 1943, Gens persuaded the Germans to ship workers to Estonian labor camps, thereby saving them at least temporarily from death. Gens could have joined his wife and daughter in hiding outside the ghetto but he refused. On September 14, 1943, Gens was shot by the Gestapo. The ghetto was completely liquidated ten days later. *–www.yadvashem.org*

12 Forced into Vilna Ghettos

Vilna Ghetto Gate *deathcamps.org*

Vilna Ghetto Street *deathcamps.org*

[13]**Vaivara** a concentration and transit camp in northeast Estonia. It was established in 1943 as a camp for Soviet prisoners of war. From August 1943 until February 1944 it was the main branch of 20 forced labor camps located throughout Estonia. Some 20,000 Jews from Latvia and from the Lithuanian ghettos of Vilna and Kovno were brought to Vaivara, where they were kept before being sent on to the labor camps. For that reason, Vaivara was considered a transit camp.

In addition, as a concentration camp, Vaivara housed 1,300 prisoners at a time. These prisoners were mainly Jews, with smaller groups of Russians, Dutch, and Estonians.

The camp commandant was SS—*Hauptsturmfuhrer* Hans Aumeier. The camp was directed by *Hauptscharfuhrer* Max Dahlmann, *Hauptscharfuhrer* Kurt Panike, and *Lagerfuhrer* Helmut Schnabel; the chief physician was Franz von Bothmann. The entire administrative staff was made up of SS *totenkopfverbande* (Death's - Head Units). The camp was guarded by an Estonian SS unit.

The prisoners worked from morning to night at different types of hard labor, such as constructing railways, digging antitank ditches, quarrying large stones and pounding them to gravel, and felling trees in forests and swamp areas where they stood up to their knees in half- frozen water. The daily food ration received by the prisoners consisted of seven ounces (200 g) of bread with margarine or ersatz jam, ersatz coffee, and vegetable soup.

After their labor and at night, the prisoners huddled together in wooden huts with very thin walls. Each hut was divided into five sections, with 70 or 80 prisoners in each section, sleeping in triple-tier rows. Water was inadequate, and washing was allowed only infrequently. Consequently, lice and disease were rife in the camp. The sick and the weak among the Jewish prisoners, and all the old people and children who could not work, were killed after *Selektionen*. The first *Selektion* was held in the fall of 1943 on the parade ground of the camp: 150 Jewish men and women who had been found unfit for labor were transferred by truck to the nearby forest and shot. In the second Selektion about 300 Jews were taken out to their death, in particular those suffering from typhoid. In twenty other *Selektionen*, held approximately every two weeks, about 500 Jewish prisoners were killed. In one *Selektion*, the children, who until then had been kept together in a special hut, were killed. Many scores of other prisoners were killed and wounded by the blows and punishments of the SS. As the Red Army approached, several hundred of the remaining prisoners were taken from the Vaivara camp westward to Saki.

In 1968, *Lagerfuhrer* Helmut Schnabel stood trial, and was sentenced to sixteen years' imprisonment; the following year his sentence was reduced to six years. Hans Aumeier was sentenced to death in Kraków and executed on December 22, 1947. —*www.jewishvirtuallibrary.org*

The electrified barbed-wire fence that separated the barracks from the water ditch surrounding the camp. Along the yard were the barracks and watchtowers. A US GI pictured this photograph.
—*motlc.learningcenter.wiesenthal.org*

[14]**Hans Aumeier** born August 20, 1906. He was an official in Nazi Germany. He was an early member of the Nazi Party, joining in December 1929, and in 1931 he joined the SA and was soon employed as a driver at the SA headquarters in Berlin. Later in December 1931 he was transferred to the SS where he worked in the garage as a driver, and was on the staff of *Reichsführer*-SS Heinrich Himmler. He had now found a job he liked and the discipline of the SA and SS suited Aumeier well, he felt he belonged, although he wanted to be a soldier. He achieved the rank of SS-*Hauptsturmführer*. He served in Dachau, Esterwegan, Lictenburg, Buchenwald, Flossenburg, Auschwitz, and Riga. He had overseen the construction of Vaivara Concentration Camp and returned there as the commander of the Vaivara concentration camp. In August 1944, when the remaining prisoners at Vaivara were sent to Stutthof, Aumeier accompanied them. In January 1945, he took over KL Grini near Oslo in Norway.

On June 11,1945, Aumeier was arrested at Terningmoen camp, he was still in full SS uniform without forged papers and admitted almost immediately his name and rank; in fact, he hid nothing. He was interrogated by U.S. intelligence officers at Akershus Prison in August 1945. In 1946 he was extradited to Poland to face trial as a war criminal along with thirty-nine other members of the SS staff of Auschwitz-Birkenau, before the Supreme National Tribunal in Kraków The trial lasted from November 25 to December 16, 1947, and Aumeier stated that if he was found guilty and sentenced to death he would "die as a *Sundenbock* (scapegoat) for Germany." He told the court that he had never killed anyone at Auschwitz and neither had any of his men and denied knowledge of the gas chambers. On December 22, 1947, Aumeier was sentenced to death, and he was hanged on January 28, 1948, in Montelupich Prison, Kraków.

—en.wikipedia.com; *jewishvirtuallibrary.org*

[15] **Organize** To "organize" meant to steal but to steal to save one's life, family members, or friends. It also means to get food, etc. from the black market. This term appears in other Holocaust memoirs, for example in *Five Chimneys* and *Playing for Time*.

[16]**Typhus** an ongoing problem in concentration camps because of primitive sanitary conditions and chronic overcrowding.

Typhus, epidemic: "A severe acute disease with prolonged high fever up to 40° C (104° F), intractable headache, and a pink-to-purple raised rash, due to infection with a microorganism called *Rickettsia prowazekii*. Among the other signs and symptoms of the disease are cough, dyspnea (difficulty breathing), vomiting, splenomegaly (enlargement of the spleen), hypotension (low blood pressure), and neurologic abnormalities including seizures, coma, and mental confusion.

R. prowazekii is found worldwide. It is transmitted by the human body louse (Pediculus humanus corporis). The lice become infected on typhus patients and transmit the illness to other people.

The mortality rate from epidemic typhus increases with age. Over half of untreated persons age 50 or more die but people of all ages can perish of the disease." Anne Frank died of epidemic typhus in the *Bergen-Belsen* concentration camp.

"The neurologic features gave the disease its name from the Greek word typhos, which means smoke, cloud, and stupor arising from fever. Epidemic typhus is also known as classic typhus, European typhus, jail fever, louse-borne typhus, ship fever." *—www.medterms.com*

[17]**Body lice** "relatively rare among affluent members of industrial nations, yet they can become a severe problem under crowded and unsanitary conditions, such as war and natural disasters. Body lice may transmit several disease agents—most notably, *Rickettsia prowazeki*, the agent of epidemic typhus." *–www.medscape.com*

[18] **The Partisans of Vilna**

A group of the partisans of Vilna: Sender, wearing a cap and with a shadow on his face, is in the second row, behind the middle partisan in the cap with the rifle. —From the back cover of the DVD *The Partisans of Vilna*, an awarding winning documentary.

[19] **Death Marches** Near the end of the war, when Germany's military force was collapsing, the Allied armies closed in on the Nazi concentration camps. The Soviets approached from the east, and the British, French, and Americans from the west. The Germans began frantically to move the prisoners out of the camps near the front and take them to be used as forced laborers in camps inside Germany. Prisoners were first taken by train and then by foot on "death marches," as they became known. Prisoners were forced to march long distances in bitter cold, with little or no food, water, or rest. Those who could not keep up were shot.

"The largest death marches took place in the winter of 1944-1945, when the Soviet army began its liberation of Poland. Nine days before the Soviets arrived at Auschwitz, the Germans marched 60,000 prisoners out of the camp toward Wodzislaw, a town thirty-five miles away, where they were put on freight trains to other camps. About one in four died on the way.

The Nazis often killed large groups of prisoners before, during, or after marches. During one march, 7,000 Jewish prisoners, 6,000 of them women, were moved from camps in the Danzig region bordered on the north by the Baltic Sea. On the ten-day march, 700 were murdered. Those still alive when the marchers reached the shores of the sea were driven into the water and shot.

The evacuations of the concentration camps had three purposes:

(1) SS authorities did not want prisoners to fall into enemy hands alive to tell their stories to Allied and Soviet liberators

(2) The SS thought they needed prisoners to maintain production of armaments wherever possible

(3) Some SS leaders, including Himmler, believed irrationally that they could use Jewish concentration camp prisoners as hostages to bargain for a separate peace in the west that would guarantee the survival of the Nazi regime.

In the summer and early autumn months of 1944, most of the evacuations were carried out by train or, in the case of German positions cut off in the Baltic States, by ship. As winter approached, however, and the Allies reached the German borders and assumed full control of German skies, SS authorities increasingly evacuated concentration camp prisoners from both east and west on foot." —www.ushmm.org

[20] **Post-war Pogroms** After World War II when some Jews returned to their homes, they were murdered. One example is the pogrom at Kielce, which refers to the events on "July 4, 1946, in the Polish town of Kielce, when 39 Polish Jews were massacred and 82 wounded out of about 200 Holocaust survivors who had returned home after World War II. Among the victims were also two non-Jewish Poles. While far from the deadliest pogrom against the Jews, the pogrom was especially significant in post-war Jewish history, as the attack took place fourteen months after the end of World War II, well after the Nazis were defeated and the extent of the Holocaust was well known to the world.

The brutality of the Kielce pogrom put an end to the hopes of many Jews that they would be able to resettle in Poland after the end of the Nazi regime. In the words of Bożena Szaynok, a historian at Wrocław University:

> 'Until July 4, 1946, Polish Jews cited the past as their main reason for emigration. After the Kielce pogrom, the situation changed drastically. Both Jewish and Polish reports spoke of an atmosphere of panic among Jewish society in the summer of 1946. Jews no longer believed that they could be safe in Poland. Despite the large militia and army presence in the town of Kielce, Jews had been murdered there in cold blood, in public, and for a period of more than five hours. The news that the militia and the army had taken part in the pogrom spread as well. From July 1945 until June 1946, about fifty thousand Jews passed the Polish border illegally. In July 1946, almost twenty thousand decided to leave Poland. In August 1946 the number increased to thirty thousand. In September 1946, twelve thousand Jews left Poland.'" —*en.wikipedia.org*

See *Fear: Anti-Semitism after Auschwitz* by Jan T. Gross

[21]**UNRRA** "The United Nations Relief and Rehabilitation Administration (UNRRA) was created at a 44-nation conference at the White House on November 9, 1943. Its mission was to provide economic assistance to European nations after World War II and to repatriate and assist the refugees who would come under Allied control.

UNRRA assisted in the repatriation of millions of refugees in 1945 and managed hundreds of displaced persons camps in Germany, Italy, and Austria during that year. It provided health and welfare assistance to the DPs, as well as vocational training and entertainment. It administered the work of 23 separate voluntary welfare agencies, including the Joint Distribution Committee, the Organization for Rehabilitation through Training (ORT), and the Hebrew Immigrant Aid Society (HIAS). In late 1945, as the displaced persons camps were given greater autonomy, the voluntary agencies increasingly operated independently. UNRRA continued to serve as a major employer of displaced persons." —*www.ushmm.org*

[22] **Joint** Since 1914, the American Jewish Joint Distribution Committee, Inc. (JDC) has served as the overseas arm of the American Jewish community. Their mission is to serve the needs of Jews throughout the world, particularly where their lives as Jews are threatened or made more difficult.

They sponsor programs of relief, rescue and renewal and help Israel address its most urgent social challenges. They are committed to the idea that all Jews are responsible for one another.

Non-Sectarian Aid – In times of crisis—natural disasters, war, famine—JDC offers aid to non-Jews to fulfill the Jewish tenet of *tikkun olam*, the moral responsibility to repair the world and alleviate suffering wherever it exists.

Their Operating Principles – JDC adheres to three operating principles:

They are non-partisan and apolitical.

They seek to empower local communities by creating model programs and training local leadership to run the programs. During a project's formative stage, they handle the administrative responsibilities and evaluate the project for effectiveness.

They build coalitions with strategic partners who, ultimately, will assume responsibility for the programs." —*www.jdc.org*

23 **Gailingen** a small German town in the district of Konstanz in Baden-Württemberg in Germany. It is situated in the southern part of the landscape called Hegau in a unique location on the northern bank of the Rhine River (High Rhine) just across from Switzerland and close to the Lake of Constance. It is therefore also called Gailingen am *Hochrhein* ("G. on the Upper Rhine"). The population currently is 3070.

Founded over 1,000 years ago, Gailingen was first mentioned in a document in 965 A.D. However, the village probably dates back to the 5th century when the Alamanni settled in the area. The name "Gailingen" literally refers to "the people of Geilo," one of the Alamanni leaders.

Beginning in the mid-17th century, Gailingen became the home of several Jewish families and gradually became one of the largest Jewish communities in the south of Germany. They built a synagogue, school, hospital and old people's home, and their population reached a number almost as high as that of the non-Jewish population. In 1870, the town elected its first Jewish mayor. Seven years later, both Jewish and non-Jewish children were attending the same school. Members of both faiths were living together peacefully until Hitler's rise to power led to the complete destruction of life as it had been for all Germans. In October 1940, over 200 Jews from Gailingen were torn out of their homes to be deported to France and then to Auschwitz.

In 1950, Gailingen became the seat for a rehabilitation clinic, and in 1972, a second one specifically addressing young people followed. A new church and a new school were built as well. What used to be a largely agricultural village is now a modern town, catering to tourists from all over the world. Due to its beautiful location, clean air, and peaceful surroundings Gailingen was awarded the title "national health resort" in 1977.
—*en.wikipedia.org*

"In the annals of Jewish history in southern Germany the town of Gailingen is unique. In the 1860s it had more Jewish than Christian inhabitants (about 1,000 each) and a Jewish mayor. Leopold Guggenheim guided the fate of the entire community from 1870 to 1884. The social service facilities in Gailingen included several Jewish institutions of trans-regional importance, in particular the Jewish hospital, built in 1891 (today, an apartment building on Büsinger Strasse 6), and **the *Friedrichsheim* Senior Citizen Home, which served elderly Jews until 1940**. The building at Gottmadinger Strasse 1 is still an old-age home. The cemetery, enlarged several times since its dedication in 1676, became one of the largest Jewish burial grounds in Baden-Württemberg; it was reopened in 1945. The synagogue, however, fell victim to the 1938 raids. Today its site, a memorial park on Ramsener Strasse, bears memorial stones. Immediately next to it was the Jewish school. It included apartments for the rabbi and religious instructor; the basement had a *mikve*.

The Jewish school and the Jewish rabbi's house, as well as the underground *mikve*, have been restored as a museum documenting Jewish life." —*www.in-gailingen.de.*

Postcard of Gailingen   circa 1900   wikipedia.com

Gailingen, Germany, 20 October 1940, Jews during deportation to Gurs, in Vichy, France, and from there to Auschwitz-Birkenau.   —yadvashem.org

View of the Gailingen displaced persons camp, [Baden] Germany 1945 - 1947.
Courtesy of William Begell *ushmm.org*

[24] ***Bar Mitzvah* or *Bat Mitzvah*** The term *bar mitzvah* literally means "son of a commandment," and *bat mitzvah* means "daughter of a commandment." This alludes to two things:

"A *bar mitzvah* boy, typically thirteen years old, or *bat mitzvah* girl, typically twelve years old, strives to come closer to God—like a son and daughter to his or her parent.

The chief way of doing so is by keeping the commandments or *mitzvot* that God gave in the *Torah*. Indeed, perhaps the most significant occurrence on this day is that the young person becomes fully responsible for keeping the commandments of the *Torah* as of that day.

Bar and *bat mitzvahs* are typically celebrated with a festive meal, with the family and friends of the *bar mitzvah* boy or bat *mitzvah girl* on hand to celebrate their entrance into adulthood." —*www.aish.com*

[25] **Shingles** a skin rash caused by the same virus that causes chickenpox. "The virus responsible for these conditions is called *Varicella zoster*. After an individual has chickenpox, this virus lives in the nerves and is never fully cleared from the body. Under certain circumstances, such as emotional stress, immune deficiency (from AIDS or chemotherapy) or with cancer, the virus re-activates causing shingles. In most cases, however, a cause for the reactivation of the virus is never found.

Before a rash is visible, the patient may notice several days to a week of burning pain and sensitive skin. Shingles start as small blisters on a red base, with new blisters continuing to form for 3-5 days. The blisters follow the path of individual nerves that comes out of the spinal cord (called dermatomal pattern). The entire path of the nerve may be involved or there may be areas with blisters and areas without blisters. Generally, only one nerve level is involved. In a rare case, more than one nerve will be involved. Eventually, the blisters pop and the area starts to ooze. The area will then crust over and heal. The whole process may take 3-4 weeks from start to finish. On occasion, the pain will be present but the blisters may never appear. This can be a very confusing cause of local pain!

In May 2006, the U.S. Food and Drug Administration (FDA) approved the first vaccine for adult shingles. The vaccine, known as Zostavax, is approved for use in adults aged 60 and over and contains a booster dose of the chickenpox vaccine usually given to children. Tests over an initial four-year period showed that the vaccine significantly reduced the incidence of shingles in these older adults." –medicinenet.com